What's it like to be a...
POLICE OFFICER

Written by Michael J. Pellowski
Illustrated by Mena Dolobowsky

Troll Associates

Special Consultant: Officer Frank Van Leeuwe, *Firearms Instructor and Warrant Officer, Fair Lawn Police Department, Fair Lawn, New Jersey.*

Library of Congress Cataloging-in-Publication Data

Pellowski, Michael.
    What's it like to be a police officer / by Michael J. Pellowski;
illustrated by Mena Dolobowsky.
      p.   cm.—(Young careers)
    Summary: Describes how police officers are selected and trained
and examines the wide variety of tasks they perform as they protect
the public and fight crime.
    ISBN 0-8167-1811-3 (lib. bdg.)   ISBN 0-8167-1812-1 (pbk.)
    1. Police—United States—Juvenile literature. [1. Police—
Vocational guidance. 2. Vocational guidance. 3. Occupations.]
I. Dolobowsky, Mena, ill. II. Title. III. Series.
HV7922.P45 1990
363.2′023′73—dc20   89-34395

What's it like to be a...
POLICE OFFICER

"Dad!" cries Sandy. "I left my bike in the park. When I went back, it was gone. What'll I do?"

"Don't worry," says Mr. Brown. "We'll go to the police station. The police will help us look for your bike."

"Here's the station. Let's go in and tell them about your bike."

Most towns have at least one police station. Big cities have many stations. The officers at each station work in a certain part of the city.

Inside the station is a big room. A police officer is behind a desk. It's Sergeant Conway. He is a desk sergeant. He helps people who come into the station.

Sandy looks worried. Sergeant Conway smiles at her. "Can I help you?" he asks.

Microphone

Fingerprint Room

Desk Railing

Lieutenant's Office

Sergeant Conway

301

Sandy tells about the missing bike. The
sergeant gives Mr. Brown a form to fill out.
He asks Mr. Brown to write down what the bike
looks like, and where and when it was left in
the park.

"We'll try to find your bicycle," Sergeant Conway promises.

Sandy smiles. "Thanks, Sergeant," Sandy says. Then she adds, "It must be exciting to be a police officer."

"Sometimes it is," says the sergeant. "But the best part is being able to help people."

"How do you become a police officer?" asks Sandy.

"Many people want to be police officers," says the sergeant. "But not everyone can. It's a hard job. Police officers must protect people and their belongings. And it's the job of the police to make sure laws are obeyed." Sergeant Conway then tells Sandy about police training.

People who want to join the police force are called recruits. Recruits must be in good shape. They also must take a special test.

Flashlight

Recruits then go to a school called the Police Academy. There they learn about police work. While they are at the Police Academy, they are known as cadets.

The cadets are given their uniforms. They are also given the equipment that they will need. They must learn how to use all their equipment properly—even their police notebooks.

Two-Way Radio

Name Tag

Emblem

Police Notebook

Key Chain

Equipment Belt

Night Stick

13

Cadets learn laws and police rules. They
learn how to help someone who's been hurt.

An important part of police training is self-
defense. Cadets learn to protect themselves and
others. Stopping a mugger is part of the job. An
academy instructor shows the cadets how to do
that.

At the academy, cadets learn an important lesson. They are taught how and when to use a gun safely. Because guns are very dangerous, learning how to use one is a big responsibility.

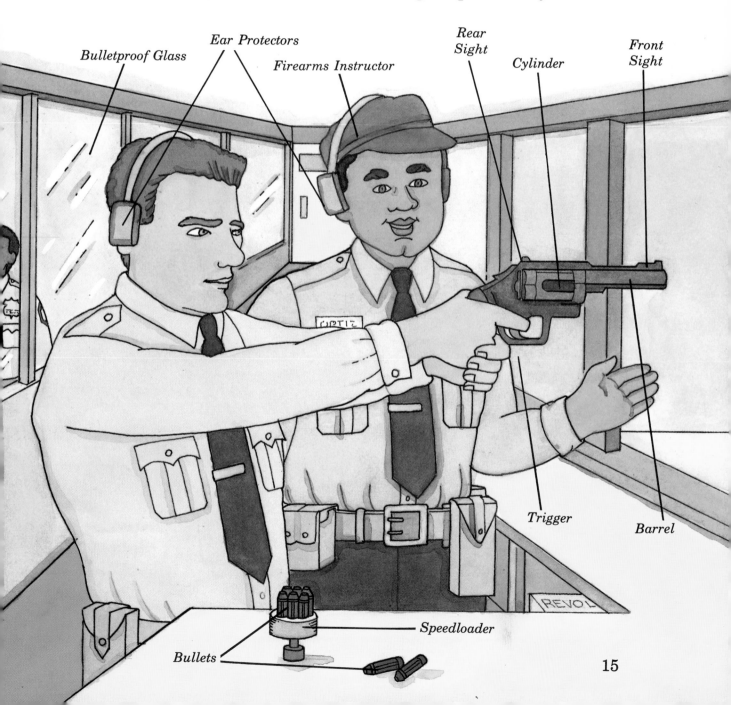

Bulletproof Glass

Ear Protectors

Firearms Instructor

Rear Sight

Cylinder

Front Sight

Trigger

Barrel

Speedloader

Bullets

Commanding Officer

Shield

Equipment Hatch

Siren

Emergency Lights

Police Rescue Vehicle

Bullhorn

"When they graduate from the academy, the new police officers have their own shields and guns," the sergeant tells Sandy. "They are assigned to police stations. Now they are ready to do real police work."

Up comes Mr. Brown. He hands the finished form to the sergeant. The officer looks it over. "Please wait," he says. "A new shift is coming in."

Police officers work different hours. The hours are called a shift. Some officers work days. Others work nights. There are always officers at the police station, ready to do their jobs.

When a shift begins, the officers check in at roll call. Next the officers gather in a place called a muster room. There each officer learns what job he or she will do during the shift.

Bulletin Board

Precinct Map

OFFICERS CHECK IN WITH DESK SERGEANT

14TH PRECINCT

1 2 3 4

RIVER

JOIN OUR TEAM

Sergeant's Stripes

Podium

Traffic Officer

Patrol Car Officer

Highway Patrol Officer

Sergeant Conway

Lieutenant

Station House Clerk

Officers are also told any important things that happened during the shift before theirs. Then each officer goes to his or her assignment.

"Look at all the officers," says Sandy, as they watch the new shift come in. "Will they *all* look for my bike?"

Mr. Brown laughs. "No," he answers. "There are many kinds of police officers. They do many different jobs."

Police
Call Box

Radio
Microphone

Emergency
Lights

Car
Identification Number

Some police officers walk a beat. They protect
a certain neighborhood in a city or town. Others
ride in patrol cars. They, too, watch a special
area.

Motorcycle police patrol the highways. They make sure drivers follow traffic laws.

WHIRRR! A siren sounds. Someone is speeding. The officer pulls the car over.

Helmet

Windshield

Headlight

Equipment Compartment

POLICE

POLICE

Exhaust Pipe

Traffic police keep cars and trucks moving smoothly. They stop traffic so people can cross the street safely.

Mounted police ride horses. They often patrol places where officers in cars cannot go.

Traffic Vehicle

Whistle

Reflector Belt

Detectives are special police. Some do not wear uniforms like other officers, so they are called "plainclothes" police. One of their jobs is to investigate crime. They study clues to find and arrest criminals. Officers become detectives after years of police experience.

Police Barricade

Detective's Badge

25

Fingerprints

Some officers work in the police lab. They study clues, such as fingerprints.

Juvenile officers work with young people. They often visit schools to talk about safety rules.

Some police officers fly helicopters. Others are harbor police, who ride in boats. They guard docks and watch for fires on ships.

Main Rotor

Landing Gear

Tailplane

POLICE

POLICE

PIER 32

27

"Come with me," Sergeant Conway says to Sandy and her father. "This department is where we put the lost or stolen things we find."

The officer in charge of the department looks up. She reads the form and smiles.

"Someone found a bike in the park earlier today. It was brought to the police station."

Property Clerk

Computer

The officer rolls out a bicycle.

"It's mine!" Sandy shouts.

The serial number on the form matches the one on the bike.

"You can take it home," says Sergeant Conway.

POLICE DEPARTMENT

Sandy is very happy. "Thanks for everything,"
she says.

"Police officers really help people in trouble,"
Sandy says to her dad. "I think when I grow up,
I'm going to be a police officer!"